Before You Marry

My Daughter

Before You Marry
My Daughter

125 Ways

to be Good at Being a Husband

Daria MonDesire

SHIRES
PRESS

Manchester Center, Vermont

SHIRES
PRESS

4869 Main Street
P.O. Box 2200
Manchester Center, Vermont 05255
www.northshire.com/printondemand.php

Cover design by Heron Graphic Arts

ISBN: 978-1-60571-010-5
Library of Congress Control Number: 2008906970

Building Community, One Book at a Time
*This book was printed at the Northshire Bookstore, a family-owned,
independent bookstore in Manchester Center, Vermont, since 1976.
We are committed to excellence in bookselling.
The Northshire Bookstore's mission is to serve as a resource
for information, ideas, and entertainment
while honoring the needs of customers, staff, and community.*

Printed in the United States of America
using an Espresso Book Machine from On Demand Books

For Gabrielle & Faith

Dear Ben,

I know you love my daughter. Every time you look at her, every time you speak to her, I see the love in your eyes. You are blessed to have each other. She loves you every bit as much as you love her. Treasure her. Life's greatest gift is to love and be loved. Sixty years from now, may your love for each other be deeper, stronger, made unshakable by the storms you've weathered and the joys you've shared. May the promises you make become the promises you live by. And may you understand that the task you take on in becoming a husband holds the honor of being keeper of the flame. It is the age-old story between husbands and wives, ever thus and ever so. Your wife cannot be the wife she wants to be unless you are the husband she needs you to be. If you would remain the love of her life, you must cherish the life of your love.

I wish I could give you perfect answers, guarantees, one bump-free road to success. I wish I could sprinkle stardust on the two of you, wrap your smiles in sunbeams, fill all your days with unspeakable joy. I cannot. What I can do, my dear, sweet son I never had, is give you this book. It holds one *woman's ideas, one wife's musings on how a good husband conducts himself. Read it. Ponder it. Turn to it from time to time. Within you lies the ability to soar. You can grace your marriage with the kind of husband most wives only dream of. May you open your mind to learning, as you have opened your heart to loving. And may your love lead you to understand.*

With love,

Mom

Before You Marry

My Daughter

1

Always treat your wife as if you'd just asked her to marry you, and you are hoping and praying she'll say, "Yes."

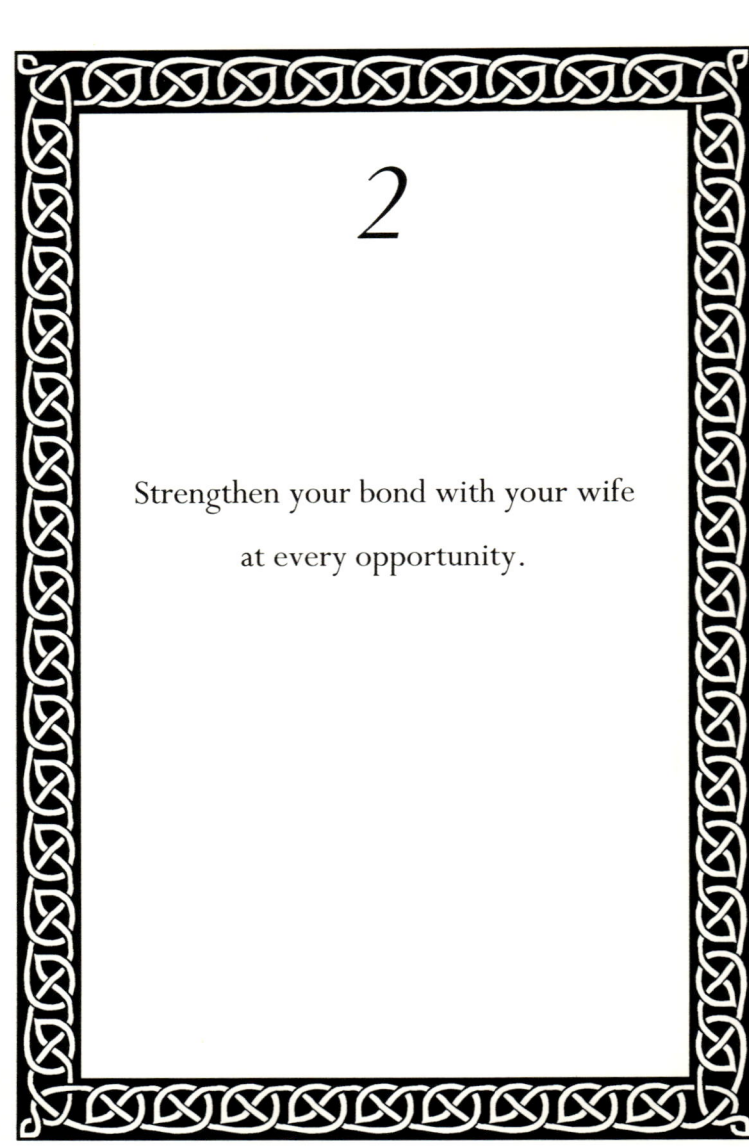

2

Strengthen your bond with your wife

at every opportunity.

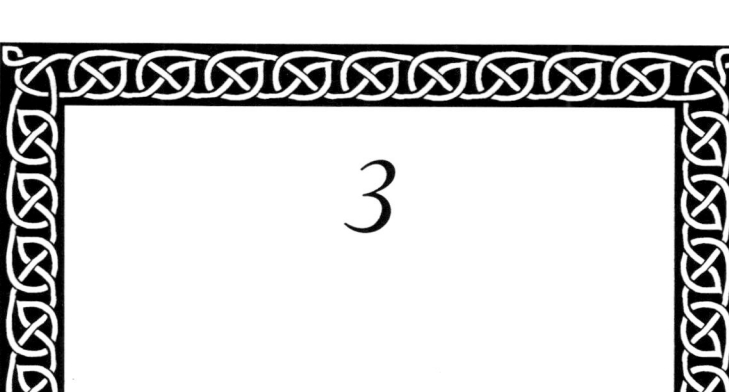

3

Let making your wife happy be

something that makes you happy.

4

If your wife tells you,
"You were disrespectful," respond
as if your house is on fire. It is.

The respect you have for your wife should be evident to everyone. It should be especially evident to your wife. If she views something you did, or said, as disrespectful, you have no time to lose. Let her know how sorry you are. Tell her how much you love and respect her. And never, *never* stand by the offending behavior.

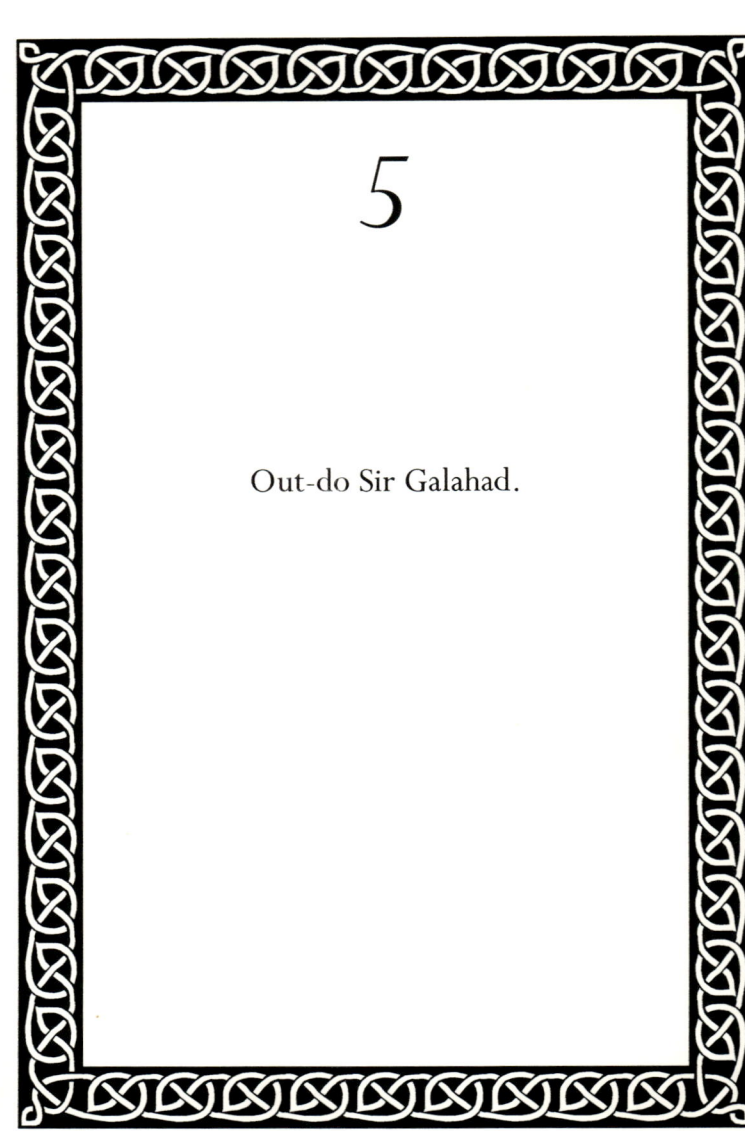

5

Out-do Sir Galahad.

6

Do not leave volatile issues on the
back burner. They will ignite.

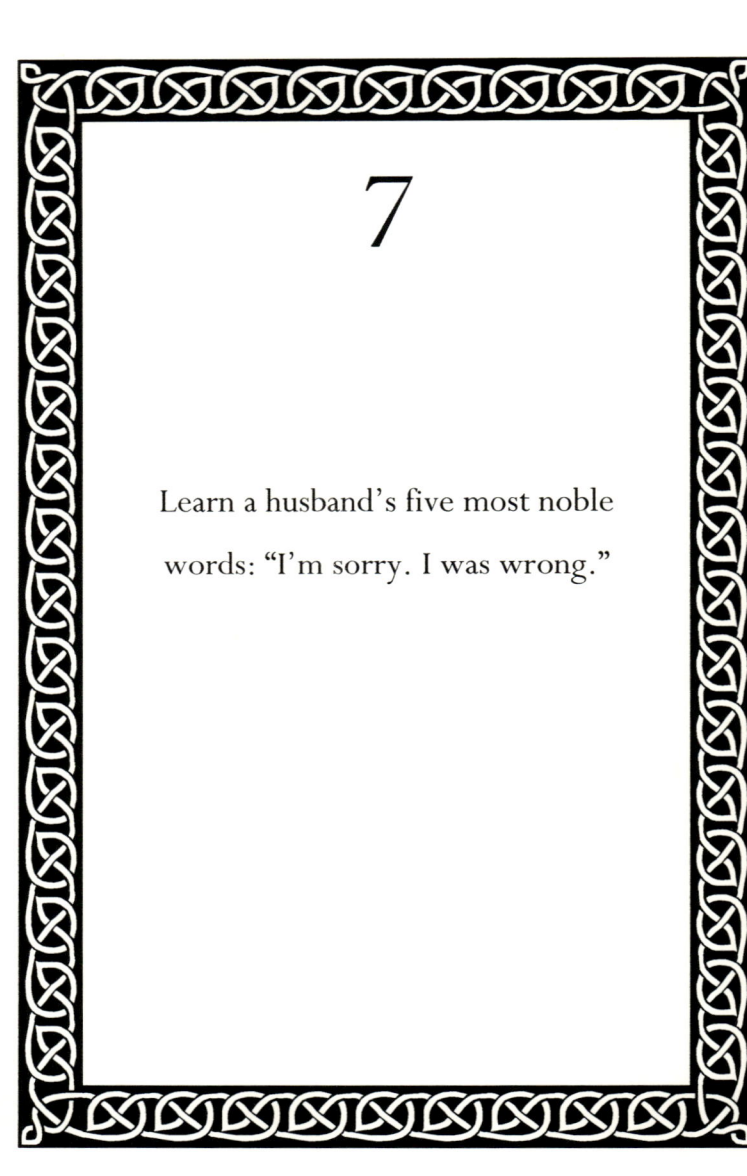

7

Learn a husband's five most noble
words: "I'm sorry. I was wrong."

8

Your wife honored you by marrying you.

Honor her.

9

How you react when your wife is upset
with you can do more damage
than what she was upset about.

Difficult as it is

to be on the receiving end

of your wife's anger,

do not criticize her;

do not attempt to justify your actions.

Make a *mega*-attempt to understand

things from your wife's perspective.

Do not tell her she's over-reacting,

being unreasonable,

making a big deal out of nothing,

or trying to pick a fight … that is,

if you don't want to turn it into a fight.

10

Stay clear of compromising situations.

11

The best thing you can do for your health

is take care of your marriage.

12

Try giving the passenger seat a try.

13

Always kiss your wife goodbye.

14

Take care of your financial obligations.

15

Never equate giving your wife the facts

with telling your wife the truth.

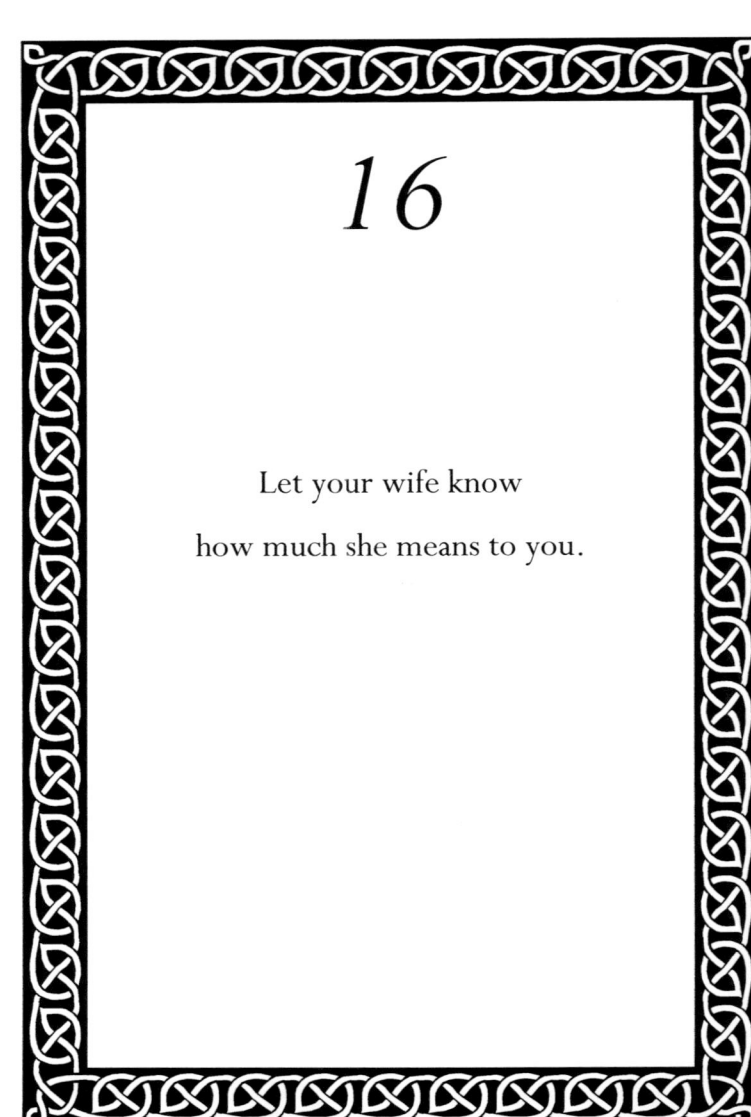

16

Let your wife know

how much she means to you.

17

Never defend indefensible behavior.

18

What your wife knows about you

is more important than

what the public believes about you.

19

The tone of your voice

carries more weight than your words.

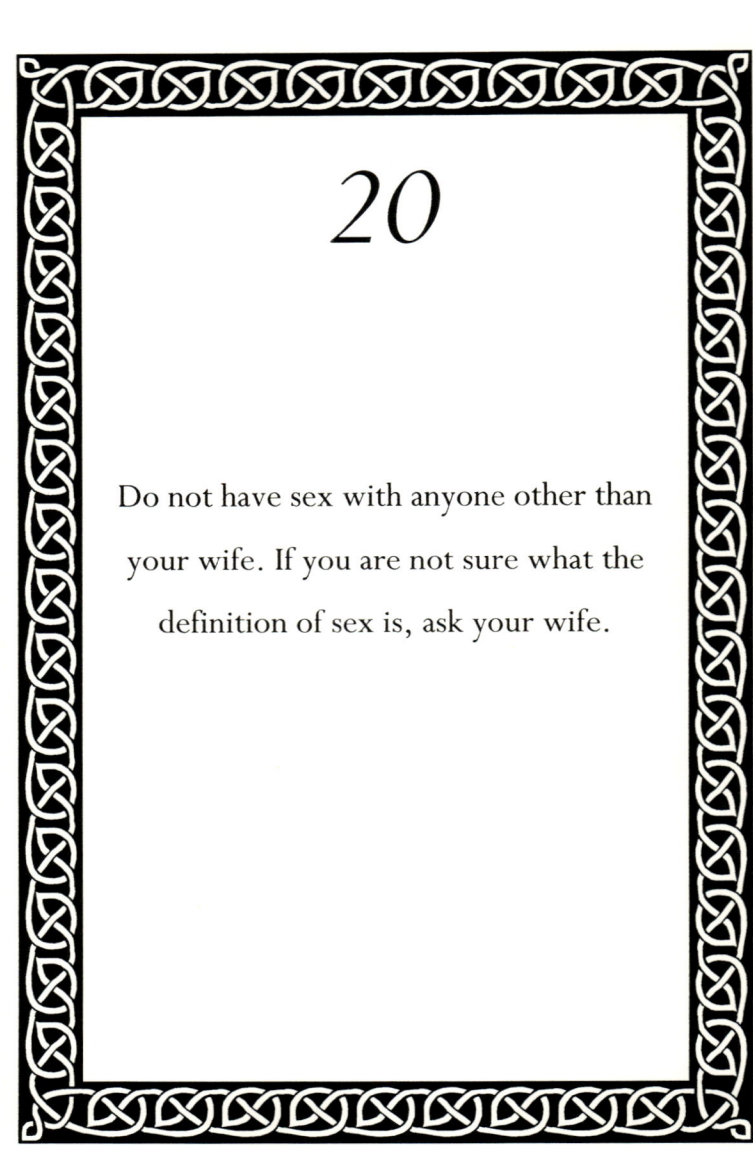

20

Do not have sex with anyone other than
your wife. If you are not sure what the
definition of sex is, ask your wife.

21

Wear your wedding ring.

22

Hurtful comments do not become okay simply because you add, "Well, you want me to be honest, don't you?"

23

Ask your wife to sit down and tell you

what's on her mind.

24

Take your wife in your arms and
dance around the house to no music.

25

Let your wife sleep late.

26

Open the new roll of toilet paper and

place it in the toilet paper holder.

27

Tell your wife you married up.

28

Splurge on a good bottle of wine.

A crazy-good bottle of wine.

Share it with your wife.

29

Take your wife to Quebec City.

30

Give your wife a shoulder rub.

31

Hold the umbrella over your wife

when it rains.

32

Cook Thanksgiving dinner.

Clean up afterward.

33

Take a shower before bed.

34

If your wife expresses discomfort
about your harmless relationship
with another woman, your relationship
with that woman is no longer harmless.

It's not about you. It's not about the other relationship. And no, it's not about trust. It's about your wife's *feelings*. If you ignore, dismiss, minimize, or disregard your wife's feelings about you and another woman, you show grave disrespect to your wife. You do serious damage to your marriage. *Don't.*

35

Tell your wife you just want to hold her.

Hold her.

36

Fix things around the house

without waiting to be asked.

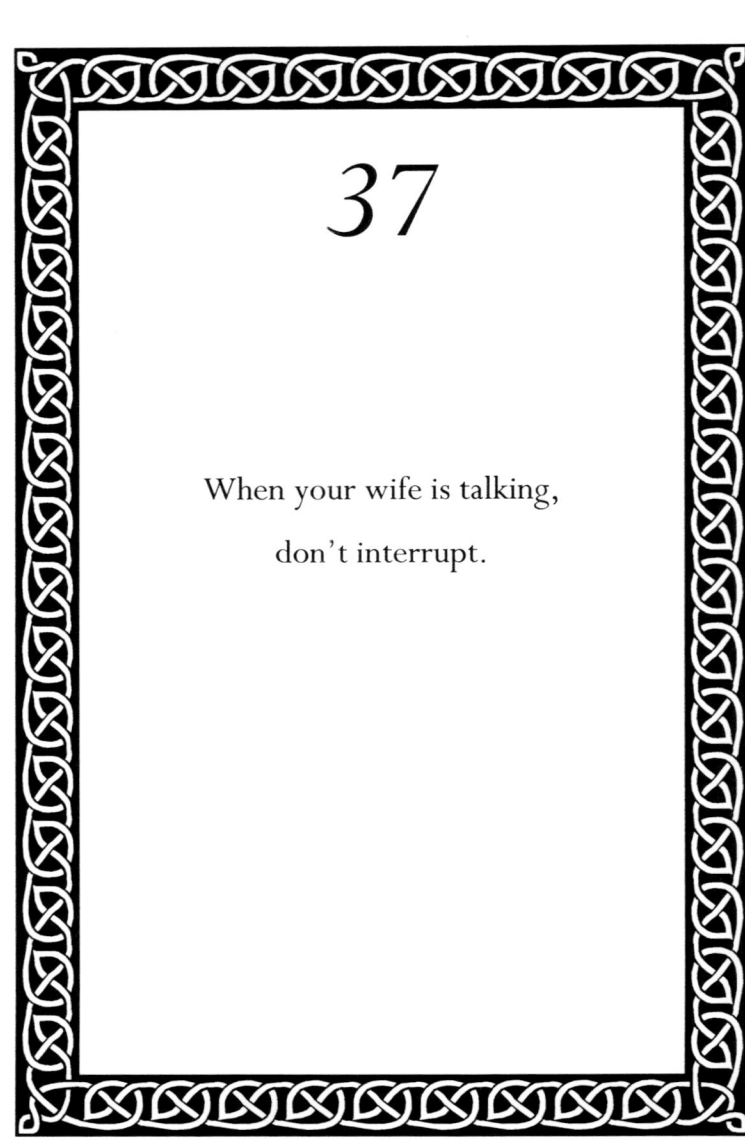

37

When your wife is talking,

don't interrupt.

38

Pick up take-out on the way home.

39

Avoid criticizing your wife's family.

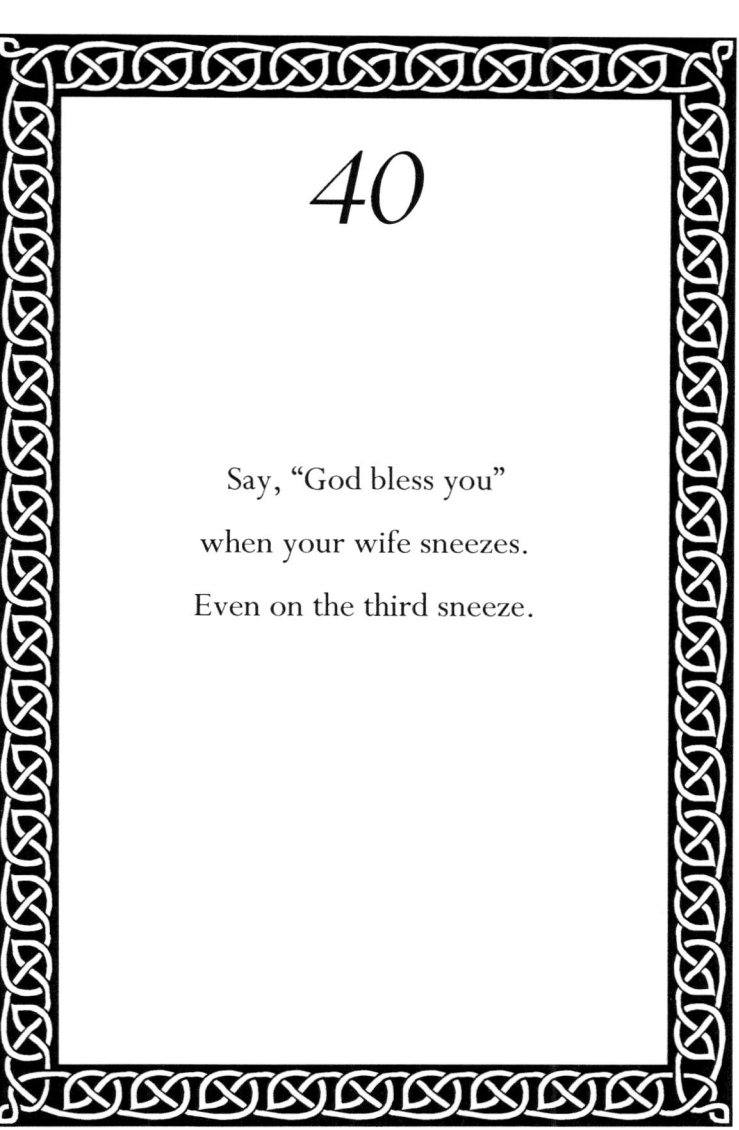

40

Say, "God bless you"

when your wife sneezes.

Even on the third sneeze.

41

Take your wife to a "Chick flick."

Share the popcorn.

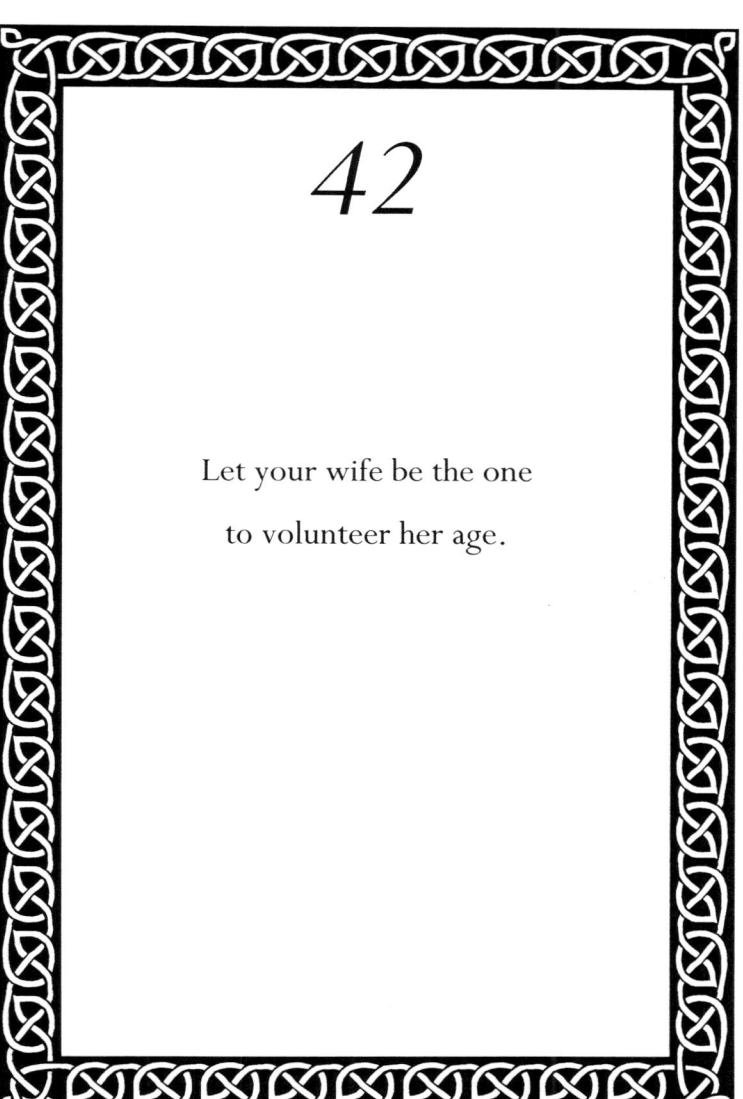

42

Let your wife be the one

to volunteer her age.

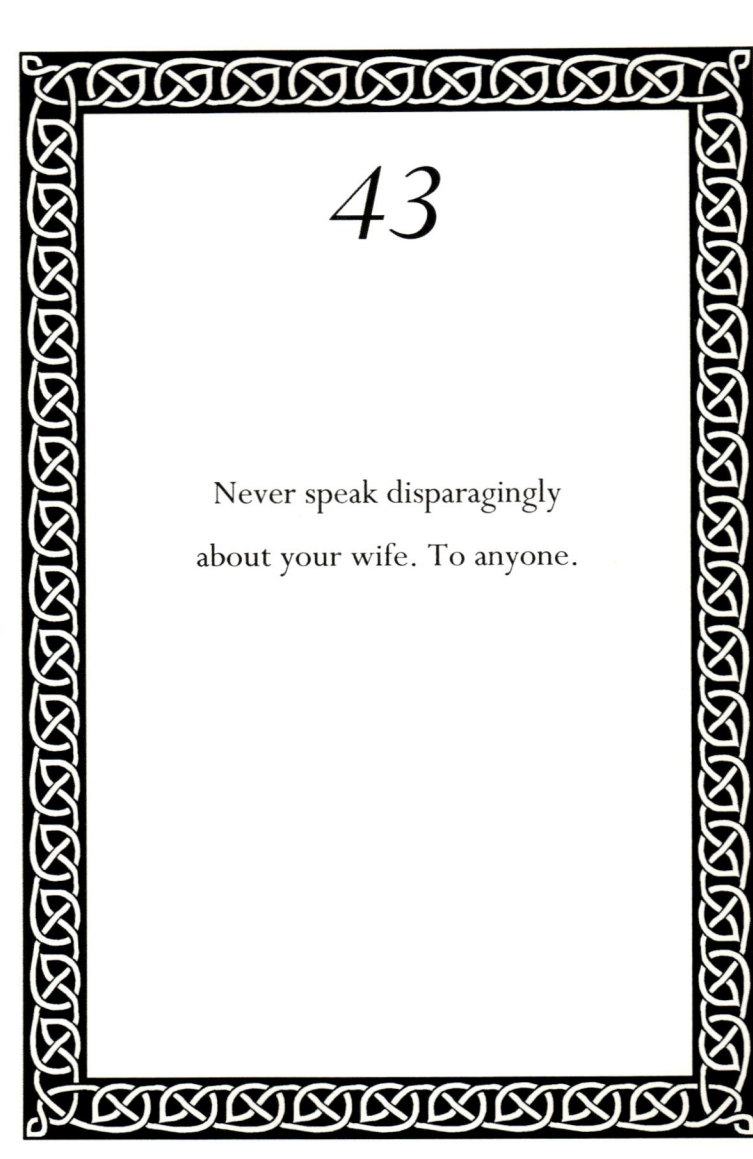

43

Never speak disparagingly

about your wife. To anyone.

44

Don't let a day go by
without telling your wife
how much you love her.

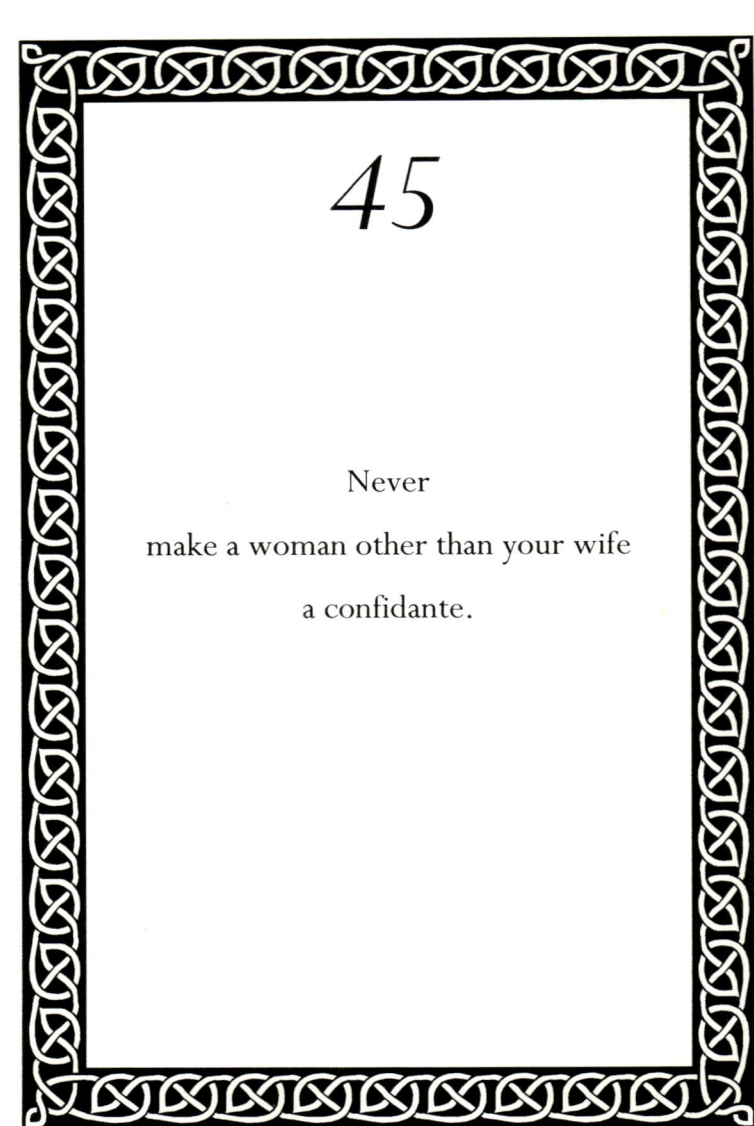

45

Never

make a woman other than your wife

a confidante.

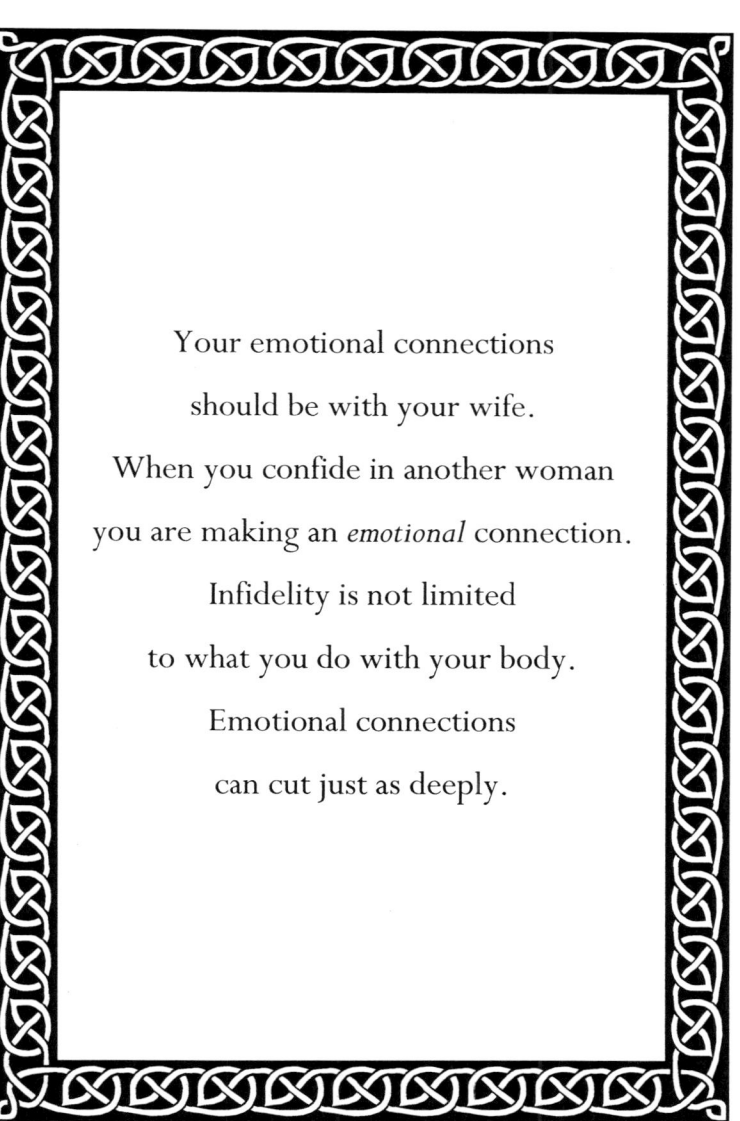

Your emotional connections

should be with your wife.

When you confide in another woman

you are making an *emotional* connection.

Infidelity is not limited

to what you do with your body.

Emotional connections

can cut just as deeply.

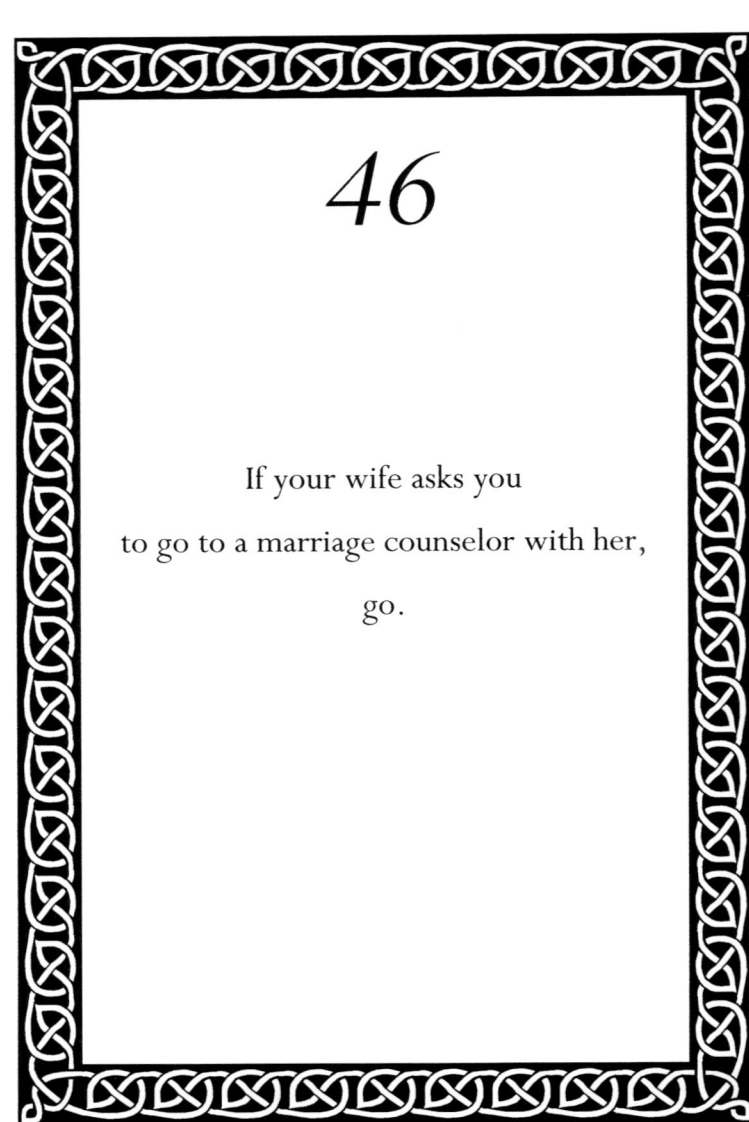

46

If your wife asks you

to go to a marriage counselor with her,

go.

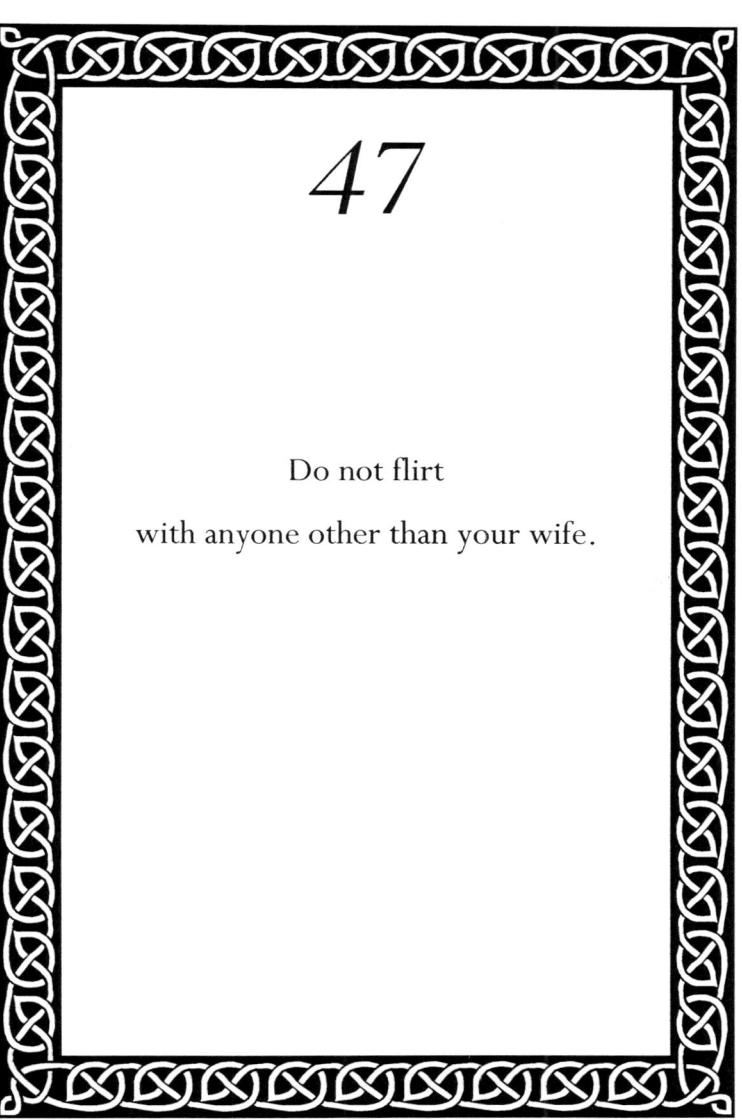

47

Do not flirt

with anyone other than your wife.

48

Flirt with your wife.

49

Give your wife

your computer password.

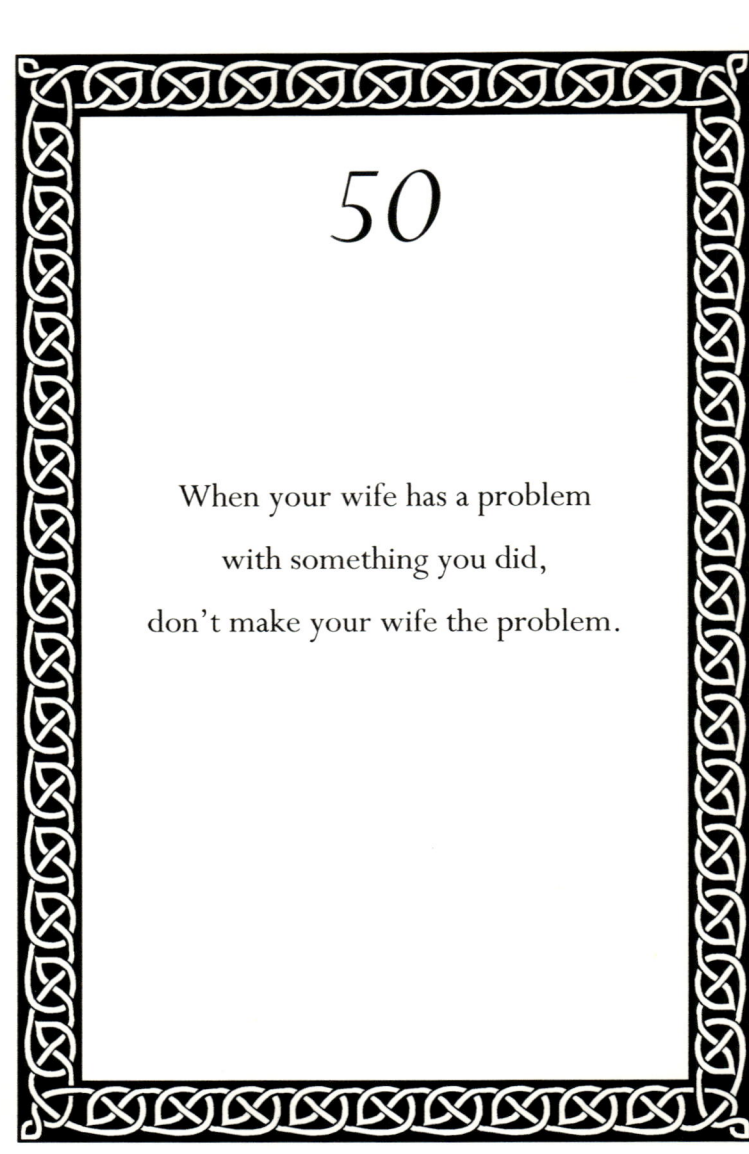

50

When your wife has a problem

with something you did,

don't make your wife the problem.

51

Draw your wife a bath. Leave.

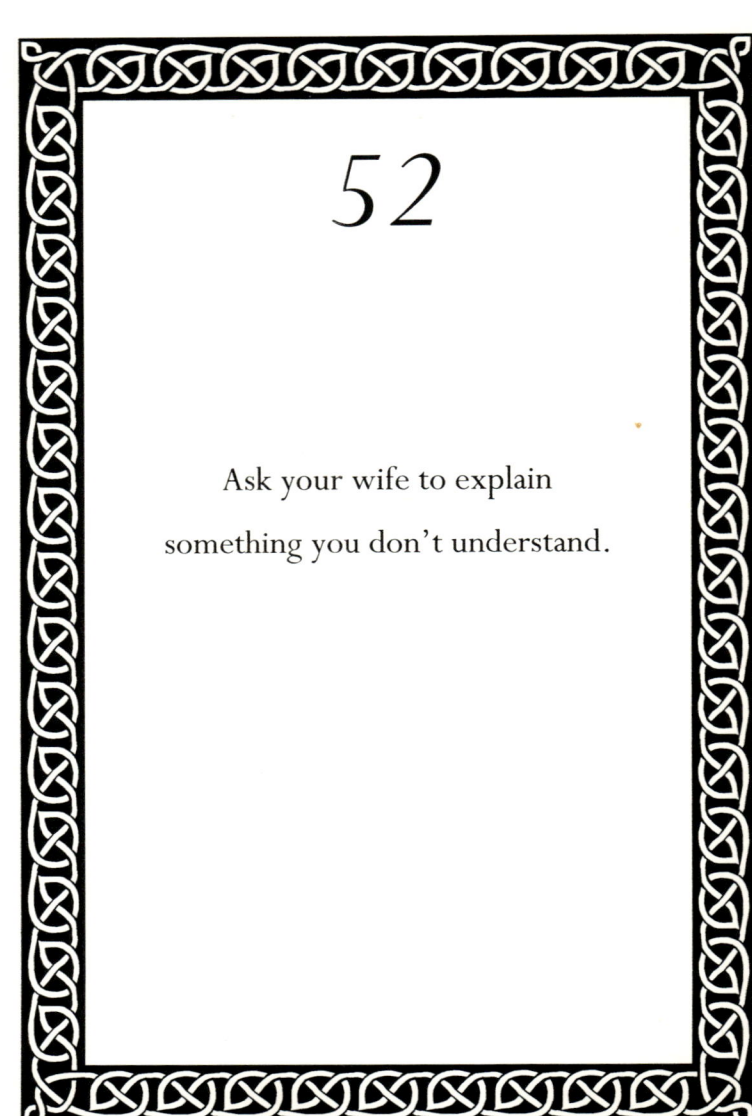

52

Ask your wife to explain

something you don't understand.

53

Get the door.

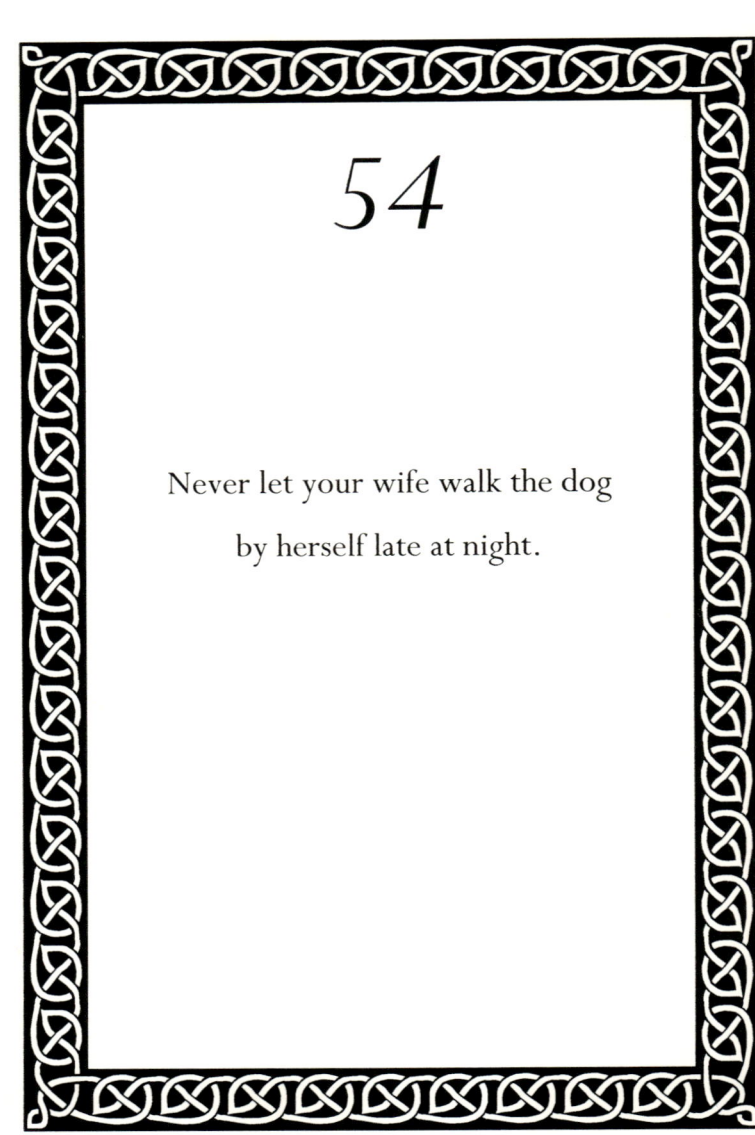

54

Never let your wife walk the dog
by herself late at night.

55

Celebrate your wife's success.

56

Give your wife a sincere,

unsolicited compliment.

57

Never talk down to your wife.

58

Not making up after a fight

can do more harm than the fight.

59

What you do when you're out of town

counts.

60

Let your wife sit down

while you dish up her food.

61

Do not throw your dirty clothes

on the bedroom floor.

62

When you're going to be late, call.

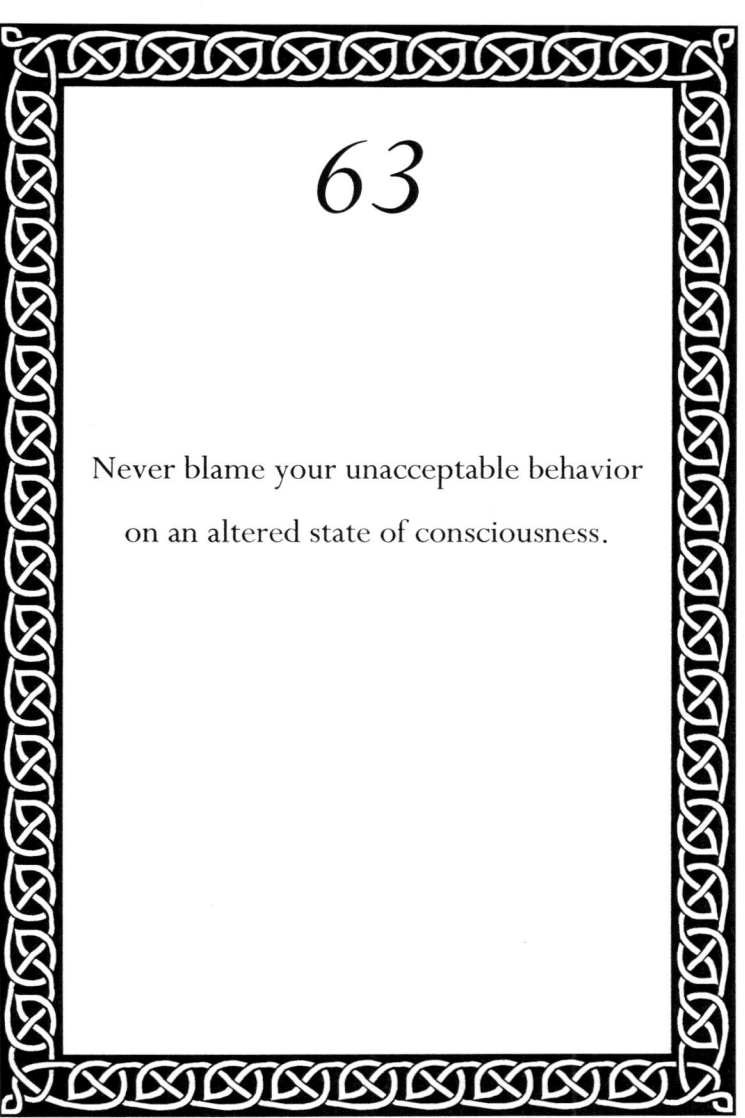

63

Never blame your unacceptable behavior

on an altered state of consciousness.

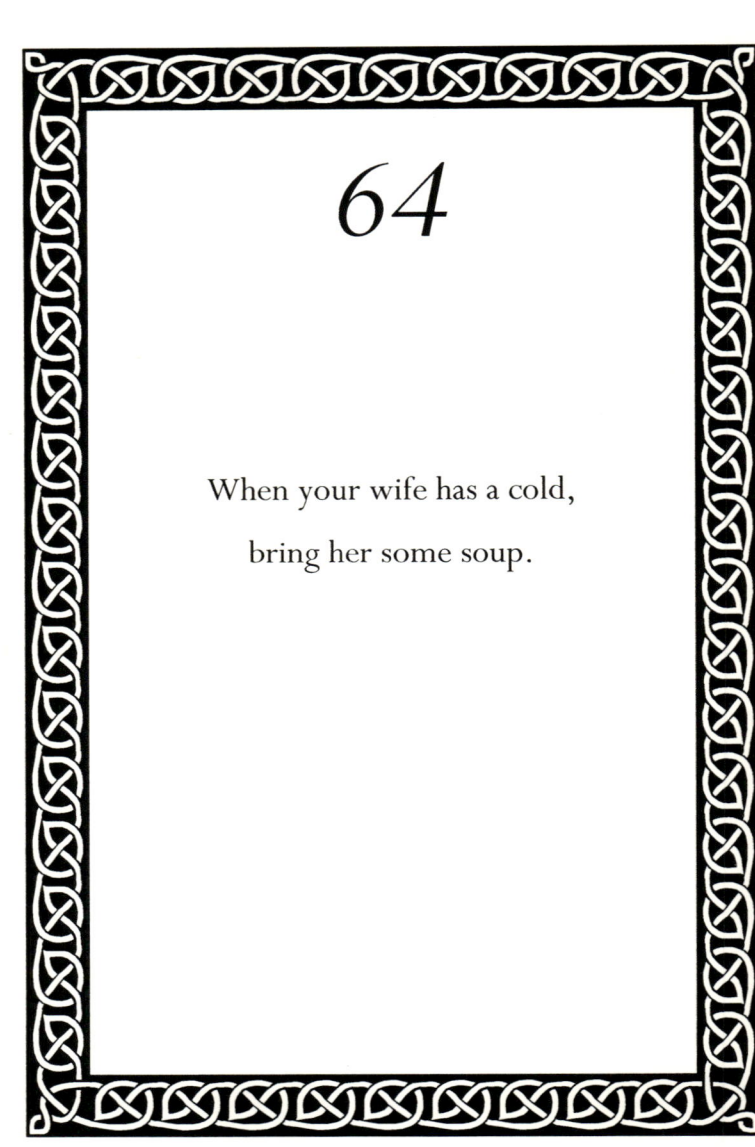

64

When your wife has a cold,

bring her some soup.

65

Go to bed early. Together.

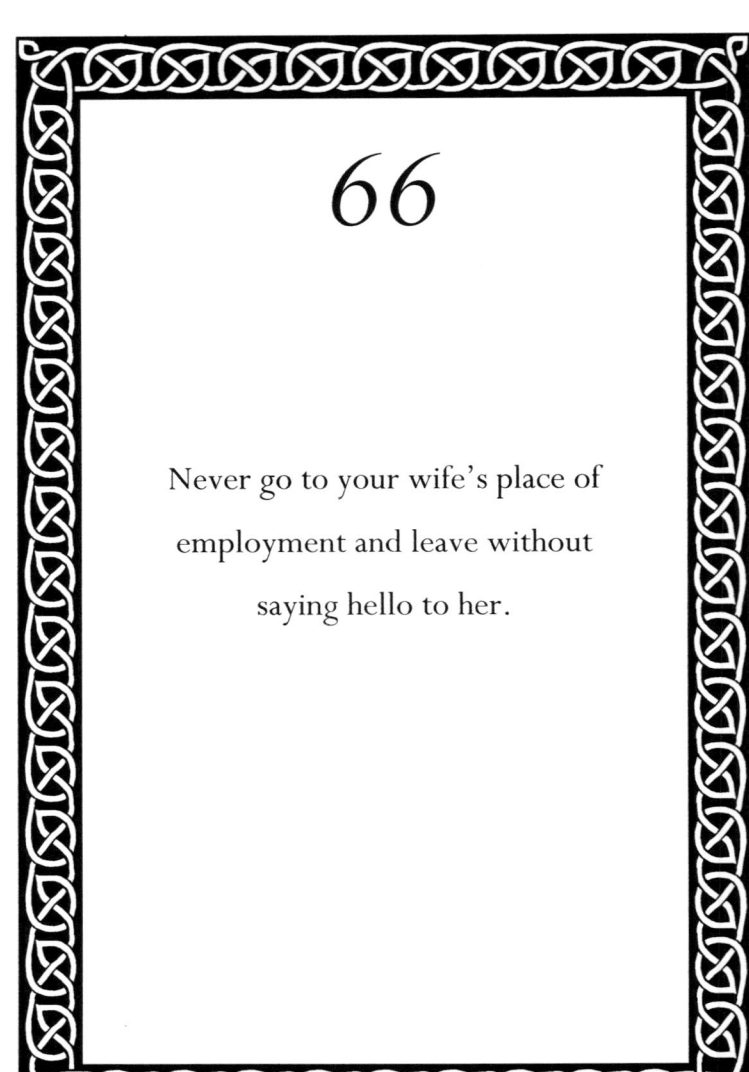

66

Never go to your wife's place of
employment and leave without
saying hello to her.

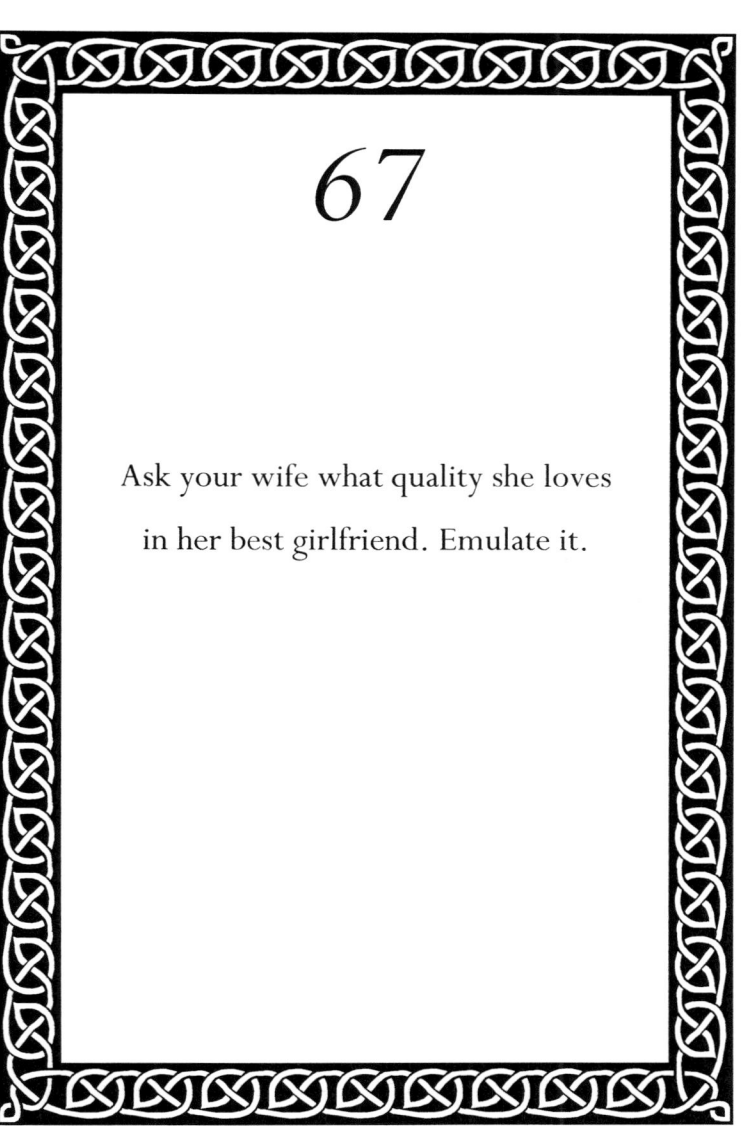

67

Ask your wife what quality she loves

in her best girlfriend. Emulate it.

68

Spend a winter weekend

in Vermont with your wife.

69

Give your wife at least four hugs a day.

70

Never drive your wife

on a trip to the country

without first checking the gas gauge.

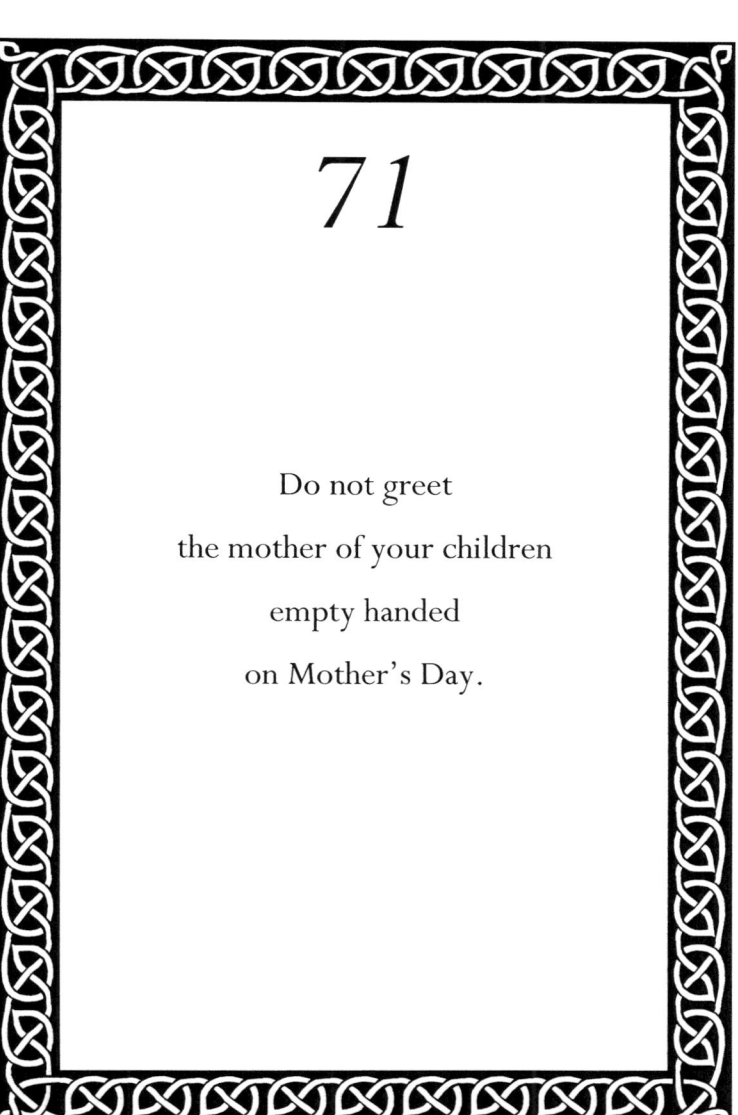

71

Do not greet

the mother of your children

empty handed

on Mother's Day.

72

Telling yourself you don't want to fight

is a good thing. Using it as a rationale

to avoid a needed discussion is not.

73

Ask your wife

what she's reading these days.

74

When your wife orders dessert, it is
neither helpful nor prudent to say,
"Do you think you really need that?"

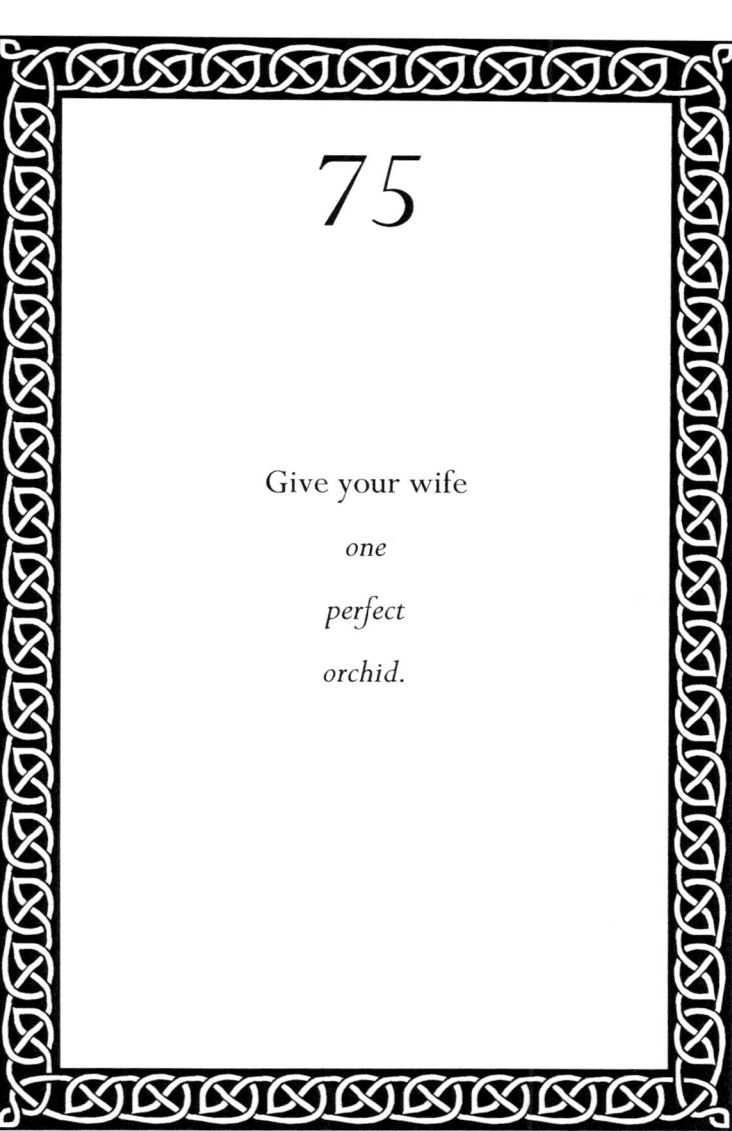

75

Give your wife

one

perfect

orchid.

76

Be aware that you cannot treat the
mother of your children disrespectfully
and still claim to be a good father.

77

Do not use the matching guest towels

in the bathroom.

78

When your wife gets annoyed, do not
attribute her annoyance to hormones.

79

Empty the grocery bags

and put the food away

even if you're not the one

who did the shopping.

80

Your sons will treat their wives

remarkably like you treat yours.

That thought should make you proud.

81

If you don't know how to fix something,

let someone who does.

82

Dig out your wife's car

after a snowstorm.

83

Ask your wife for a list of names she'd
like you to call her. Stick to the list.

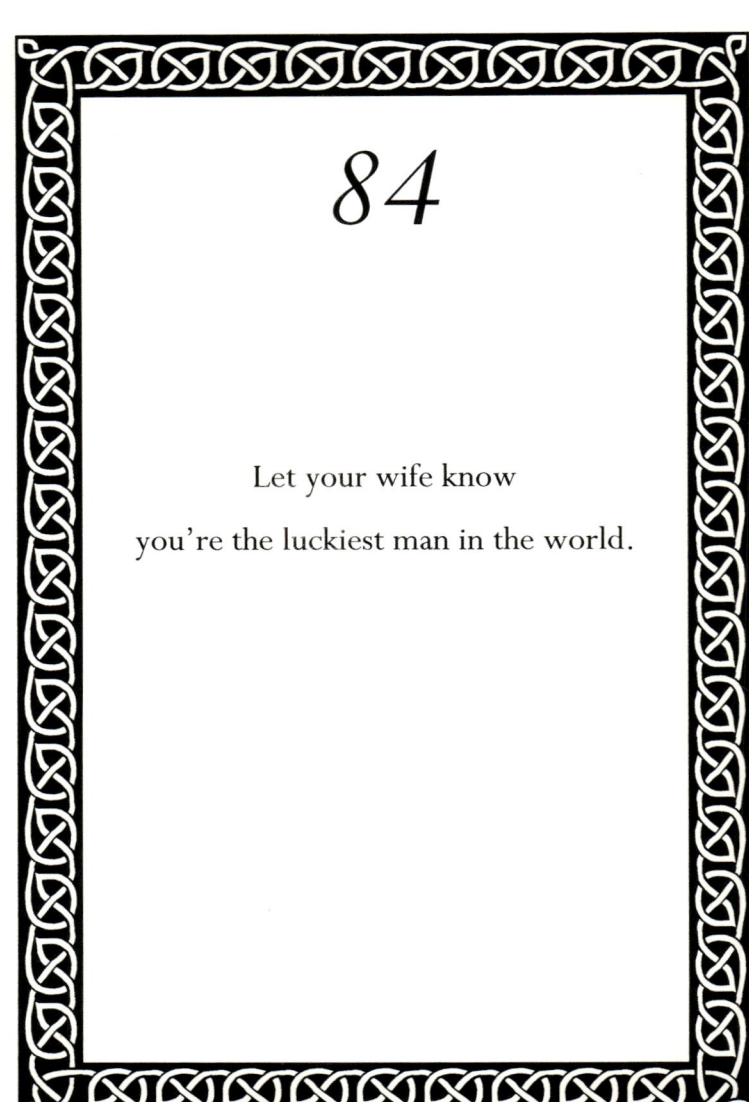

84

Let your wife know

you're the luckiest man in the world.

85

Christmas Day is December 25th.

86

It is not okay to check out other women.

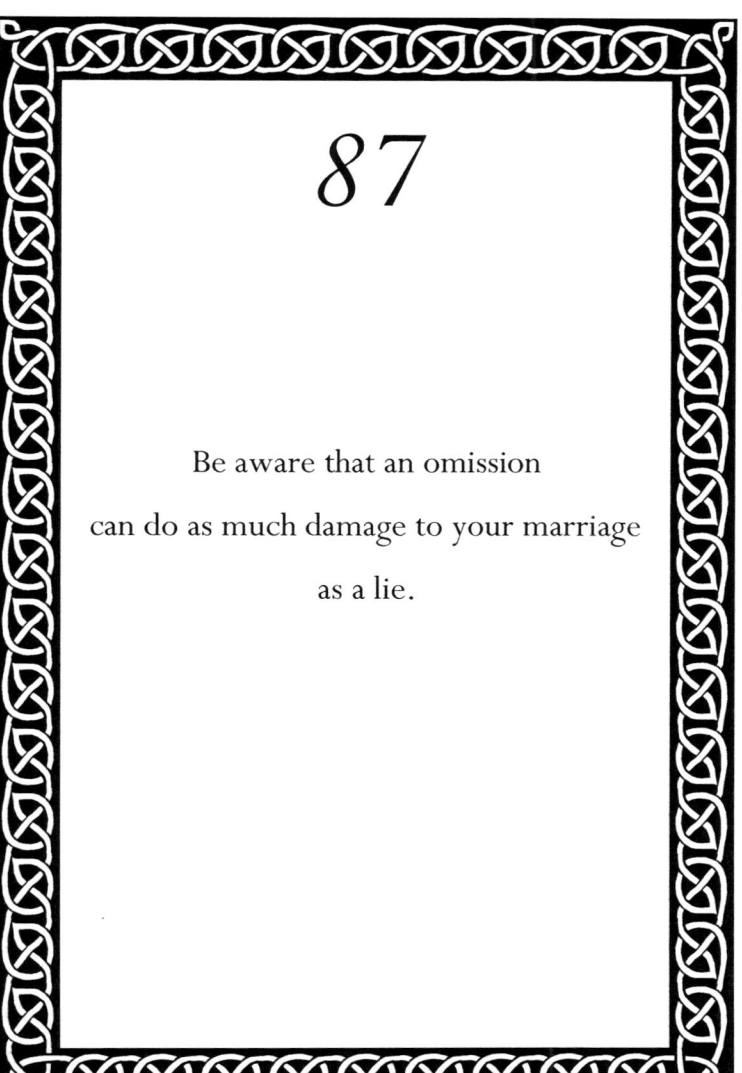

87

Be aware that an omission

can do as much damage to your marriage

as a lie.

88

Pull out your wife's chair for her.

89

If your wife goes on about a mistake you
made, she is not trying to make you feel
bad. She is trying to get you
to help her feel better.

90

When your wife is in the hospital,

bring flowers.

91

Walk hand-in-hand with your wife.

92

At the close of a phone call,

be the first to say, "Love you."

93

Never betray your wife's trust.

94

If you do not live up to the trust your
wife places in you, do not accuse
your wife of not trusting you.

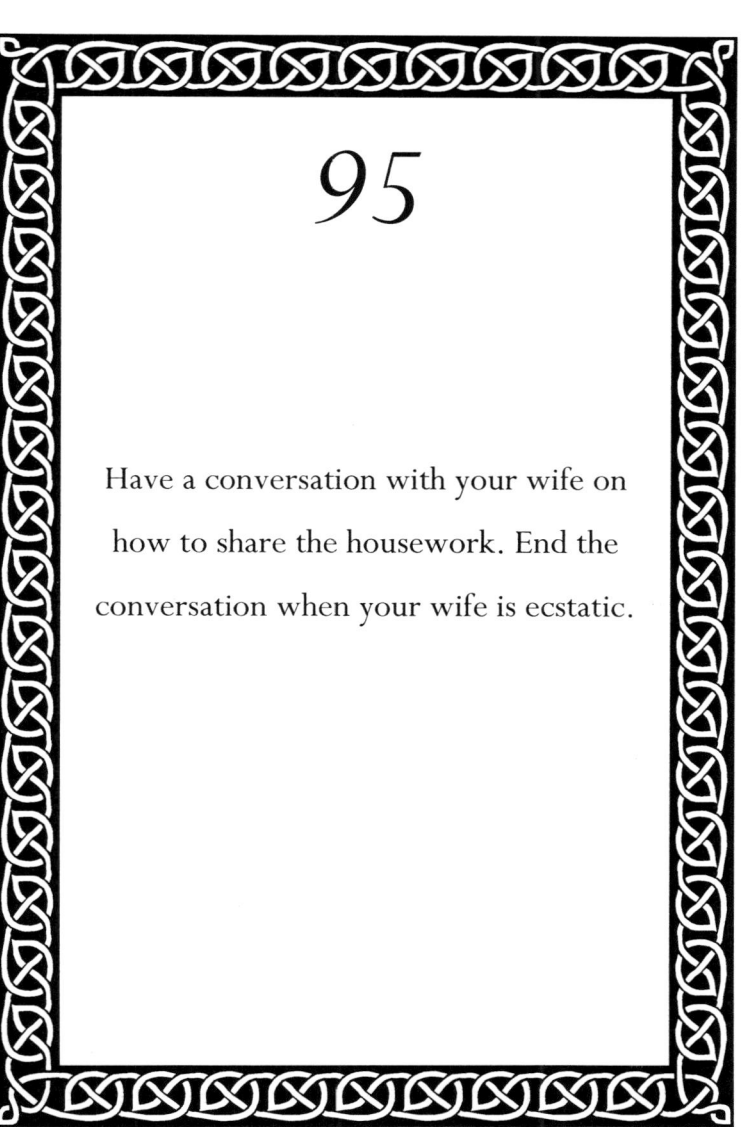

95

Have a conversation with your wife on how to share the housework. End the conversation when your wife is ecstatic.

96

Spend the night in a motel together.

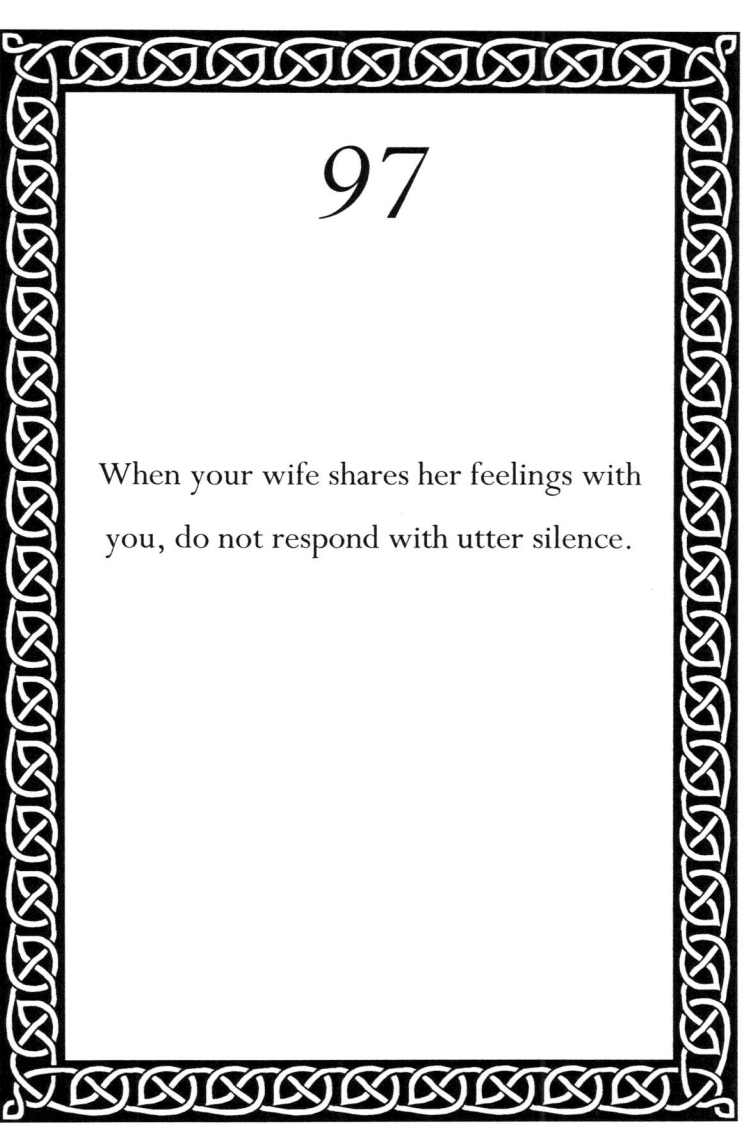

97

When your wife shares her feelings with you, do not respond with utter silence.

98

Never snap at your wife.

99

If you ever

hit, push, shove,

or hurt my daughter,

not only are you a poor excuse

for a husband, you are a

sorry excuse for a man.

100

I will find you.

101

Let your wife hog the covers.

102

To keep a good marriage from deteriorating, you must *constantly* work at making it *better*.

103

Remember your anniversary.

Write down the month, day,
and year here:

_____

104

Never take a business trip with a female
colleague over your wife's objections.

105

Your daughters will let men

remarkably like you

into their lives.

That thought should help you sleep well.

106

Open the car door for your wife.

Once she's settled, close it.

107

Watch *I Love Lucy* reruns together.

108

Bring one of your wife's hands up to your lips, and lightly kiss the back of it.

109

Never tell your wife you don't

remember telling her

you don't remember.

110

Bake your wife's birthday cake.

111

What your wife doesn't know

will hurt you.

112

When your wife asks you

to give her a hand with something,

do not refuse to help her.

113

Get a pedicure.

No, don't do it yourself.

114

Write your wife a long love letter.

Mail it.

115

If your wife asks you

if you find another woman attractive:

1. Say, "No."

2. Tell her she's the only woman

in the world for you.

3. Do not forget step 2.

116

Never allow your children

to be rude to your wife.

117

The proper position of a toilet seat

is down.

118

Kiss your wife as if kissing is all there is.

119

Listen with your heart.

Speak from your soul.

120

Sing your wife's praises to your family.

121

Do not wait until the day before
to buy your wife's gift.

122

Ask your wife if there are things

about the way you treat her

that she'd like you to change.

Change them.

123

Never confuse an explanation

with an apology.

One is silver; the other, platinum.

124

Work toward getting the "Good Husband Lifetime Achievement Award."

125

What your wife tells you she needs
from you is more important than
anything you will ever find in a book.

 *Contact the Author*

If you'd like to contact Daria MonDesire to share your thoughts on what you've read, please feel free to write to her (please enclose a SASE) at P.O. Box 892, Derby Line, Vermont 05830; or you may email her via her website: www.mondesire.com.

THE GOOD HUSBAND
LIFETIME ACHIEVEMENT AWARD

_____

has been a beacon of virtue,
and a husband of great compassion,
kindness, and loyalty; and

he has shown himself to be
a sensitive listener,
a thoughtful companion,
and a true and devoted friend; and

Whereas,

he has exemplified these qualities
year, after year, after year;

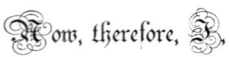
Now, therefore, I,

_____,

wife of said husband,

do hereby affirm and proclaim
that he has earned the honor
of being deemed

A GOOD HUSBAND

and of receiving

THE GOOD HUSBAND
LIFETIME ACHIEVEMENT AWARD

Presented this _____ day of _____,

in the year _____

Signed

_____

Words From the Author

We hope that you enjoyed learning about the wonderful country of Bermuda.

Bermuda is a country rich in culture and beauty, with lots of wonderful places to visit and people to meet.

We hope you continue to learn more about this wonderful nation. If you enjoyed this book, consider leaving a review!

With Love